"WHEN I WAS YOUR AGE..."

Remarkable Achievements of Writers, Artists, and Musicians at Every Age from 1 to 100

Written by David Lewman
Illustrated by Mark Anderson

TRIUMPH
BOOKS
CHICAGO

This book is available in quantity at special
discounts for your group or organization.
For further information, contact:

Triumph Books
644 South Clark Street
Chicago, Illinois 60605
(312) 939-3330 FAX (312) 663-3557

ISBN 1-57243-144-X

CONTENTS

Every year, around her birthday, my sister gets gloomy. Not because she's worried about wrinkles, but because she's a musician, and birthdays remind her of MOZART.

This is my fault. For her fifteenth birthday, I gave her a popular Mozart biography. She had known, in a general way, that young Mozart was pretty hot stuff, but now she had all the undeniable particulars.

The next year, when I wished her happy birthday, she muttered, "By 16, Mozart had already written twenty symphonies."

INTRODUCTION

"Yeah, but could he drive a car?" I asked. Every birthday after that was the same: another year for my sister, another light-year for Mozart.

"Happy 20th, Sis."

"At age 20, Mozart wrote his eighth piano concerto."

"Happy 30th."

"*Marriage of Figaro*."

Last month, after twenty years of this, I thought I finally had her. "Happy Birthday, Sis—at 36, Mozart was dead."

"Yes," she said, "but at 36, VERDI wrote *Rigoletto*."

My sister is not alone in comparing her age and accomplishments to those of the celebrated and famous. Even after he'd won the Nobel Prize, ALBERT CAMUS calculated in his journal how old TOLSTOY had been when he wrote *War and Peace*.

From earliest infancy, age is our guide to proper accomplishment: by six months, you should be able to crawl; by one year, to walk; and by two years, to talk. Once we enter kindergarten, age tells us where we should be for the next thirteen years (at least). We never shake the habit, always looking to our total number of trips around the sun to tell us what we should have accomplished.

Have we fallen hopelessly behind, or do we still have a chance to make our mark? Paradoxically, the answer is yes. We have fallen behind TOULOUSE-LAUTREC, speaking his first words at six months and sketching avidly at age 3. Behind JOHANN STRAUSS, composing his first waltz at age 6. And behind JORGE LUIS BORGES, publishing a translation at age 9. But despite these daunting acts of precocity, we can take inspiration from flowers that bloom a little later. At 44, ROBERT LUDLUM turned to writing. At 47, TCHAIKOVSKY conducted in public for the first time. At 76, GRANDMA MOSES put down her embroidery and picked up a paintbrush.

It's never too late. But it's never too early, either.

THE SINGLE DIGITS

CHILD-HOOD

KEITH JARRETT, future jazz pianist, 6 months old, learns to talk. ARTUR RUBINSTEIN, age 2, learns the piano keys by their names and can call out the notes of any chord without looking. He is, presumably, a big hit at parties. According to his Catholic mother, TOULOUSE-LAUTREC, age 2, improvises a prayer: "Good night little Jesus, I give you my little heart." RAY CHARLES, age 3, starts playing the piano. Future writer and philosopher JOHN STUART MILL begins studying Greek at age 3.

GEORGIA O'KEEFFE starts the first grade at age 4. JEAN-PAUL SARTRE, age 4, puts salt in the jam and gets caught. Maybe this is where he gets the idea that life has no meaning. HELEN REDDY, age 4, makes her singing debut at the Tivoli Theatre in Perth, Australia. She does not sing "I Am Toddler, Hear Me Squeak." STEVE MILLER, age 4, learns basic guitar chords from Les Paul (these few chords will see him through his entire career). MOZART, age 4, composes a concerto for the clavier.

JOHN LENNON
learns to read.

Age FOUR

At a talent show, BUDDY HOLLY, age 5, wins five dollars singing "Down the River of Memories." MOZART, age 5, composes several minuets. Although a poor reader and writer (and hopeless at arithmetic), PABLO PICASSO at age 5 draws remarkably accomplished sketches. CARL PERKINS, not wearing blue suede shoes, goes to work picking cotton at age 6. HELEN KELLER, age 6, learns her first word, *water*.

HENRY MILLER

uses foul language in the street
and gets pulled into the
police station by an older girl.
The desk sergeant lectures
Henry about using profanity.

Future Dadaist

MAN RAY

draws the battleship *Maine*
using every color in his
box of crayons.

PRINCE NELSON (who has not yet dropped his last name—or his first) teaches himself to play piano at age 7. MARVIN HAMLISCH is accepted by the Juilliard School of Music, at age 7 their youngest pupil ever. Violinist YEHUDI MENUHIN, age 7, solos with the San Francisco Symphony Orchestra. PAGANINI, age 7, composes his first violin sonata. GLADYS KNIGHT, age 7, wins $2,000 singing on Ted Mack's *Amateur Hour*.

On his 8th birthday, BILLY FAULKNER finally starts the first grade. ROY ORBISON, age 8, performs on local radio shows in Texas. IGGY POP, age 8, hears Frank Sinatra for the first time and realizes he wants to be a singer. CHOPIN gives his first public performance on the piano at age 8. JOHN STUART MILL, age 8, reads all of Herodotus, parts of Xenophon, and several others in the original Greek. Unfortunately, *Green Eggs and Ham* hasn't been written yet. MOZART, age 8, composes his first symphony.

JORGE LUIS BORGES, age 9, publishes his Spanish translation of Oscar Wilde's story, "The Happy Prince." BÉLA BARTÓK, age 9, composes his Opus Number One, a waltz. Under the guidance of her father, CLARA WIECK (later Clara Schumann) begins her concert career as a pianist at age 9. Coincidentally, so does FELIX MENDELSSOHN. And so does FRANZ LISZT.

JOSEPH CONRAD
puts his finger on
the blank map of Africa
and resolves to go there
when he grows up.

JONI MITCHELL
recovers from polio,
singing loudly in the
children's ward.

THE TEENS

A TRIP THROUGH ADOLES-CENCE

STEVIE MORRIS, age 10, is introduced to Motown's Berry Gordy, who renames the young virtuoso "Little Stevie Wonder." COLE PORTER, age 10, writes a one-song operetta, *The Song of the Birds*. MELISSA ETHERIDGE, age 10, writes her first song, "Don't Let It Fly Away [It's Love]." ANTOINE DOMINO, JR., age 10, plays for pennies in honky-tonk bars and soon acquires the nickname "Fats."

HANK WILLIAMS, age 11, moves to a railroad camp where he learns about country music at the Saturday night dances. BEETHOVEN, age 11, leaves school. HARRY CONNICK, JR., age 11, goes into the studio and pounds a piano for an album he'll release fourteen years later. Stopped by his father while trying to ship out to sea as a cabin boy, JULES VERNE, age 11, promises his parents that he will henceforth travel only in his imagination. JACK KEROUAC, age 11, enters an all-English-speaking school, where he struggles with the unfamiliar language.

CHARLES DICKENS

goes to work in a factory,
pasting labels on pots of shoe polish
for six shillings a week.

ANDREW WYETH, a sickly child who studies at home, spends his 12th year building a complete miniature theater for his presentation of Sir Arthur Conan Doyle's *The White Company.* Despite his evident musical talent, NIKOLAY RIMSKY-KORSAKOV, age 12, is enrolled in the St. Petersburg naval academy. ALFRED TENNYSON, age 12, writes a 6,000-line epic poem full of battles, seascapes, and mountainous scenery. DOLLY PARTON, age 12, appears at the Grand Ole Opry. JOHN DONNE, with a good command of French and Latin, goes to the University of Oxford at age 12.

CARL SANDBURG, age 13, quits school to work as a day laborer. Irish playwright SEAN O'CASEY finally learns to read and write at age 13. AUGUSTE RODIN, age 13, becomes an apprentice in a factory and learns to paint floral patterns on porcelain. JOHN PHILIP SOUSA, age 13, enlists in the Marines, serving as an apprentice in the band. JOHN COLTRANE, age 13, takes up the saxophone. BRUCE SPRINGSTEEN, after buying a second-hand guitar for eighteen dollars, becomes the first in his family, at age 13, to play an instrument.

SAM CLEMENS, age 14, joins the Cadets of Temperance, pledging not to smoke cigars for three months. ANSEL ADAMS, age 14, talks his family into vacationing at Yosemite National Park, where he receives his first camera, a Kodak Brownie, from his parents. GEORGE HARRISON, age 14, joins his friend Paul McCartney's band, the Quarry Men, led by John Lennon. JANE AUSTEN, age 14, finishes her first novel, *Love and Freindship* (sic). SONNY SALINGER, age 14, flunks out of Manhattan's McBurney School, an experience he will put to good use in *The Catcher in the Rye*.

EUBIE BLAKE, age 15, begins playing ragtime piano in a Baltimore bordello. THOMAS WOLFE, age 15, enters the University of North Carolina. PAUL ANKA, age 15, saves enough soup labels to win a trip to New York, where he auditions for ABC with his own song, "Diana," which becomes a number-one hit. JOHANN SEBASTIAN BACH, age 15, joins a poor boys' choir (the boys are poor, not the choir). EZRA POUND, age 15, resolves to know more about poetry than any man living by the time he's thirty.

CLAUDE MONET,
a grocer's son, draws caricatures
for twenty francs each.
Orders roll in.

PAUL HEWSON, age 16, and three other Dubliners start a rock band, U2, and Hewson decides to call himself Bono.

L. L. COOL J, age 16, raps his first hit single, "I Need a Beat." Apparently, though, he doesn't need a diploma; when the song takes off, he drops out of high school. BILLIE HOLIDAY, age 16, gets a job singing in a Harlem nightclub.

ELLA FITZGERALD, age 16, sings at an amateur show in Harlem's Apollo Theatre and is discovered and hired by bandleader Chick Webb. TENNESSEE WILLIAMS, age 16, publishes his first story. So does EDITH WHARTON.

In his senior year,
JACK KEROUAC
scores the winning
touchdown in Lowell High
School's big Thanksgiving
Day football game.

KURT VONNEGUT, JR., age 17, enters Cornell University as a biochemistry major to please his father, who wants him to study something useful. RICHARD STARKEY (the future Ringo Starr) receives his first drum set from his stepfather at age 17. CLAUDE DEBUSSY, age 17, fails to win a piano prize. Luckily, the composition thing works out pretty well. After one year at Mount Holyoke Female Seminary, EMILY DICKINSON, age 17, returns to her father's house, where she will spend the rest of her life. GEORGES BIZET, age 17, composes one of the best symphonies ever written by a teenager, his Symphony in C Major.

Three months shy of graduation, DUKE ELLINGTON, age 17, quits high school, where he's taken only one semester of music—and gotten a D. MENDELSSOHN, age 17, composes an astonishingly mature Overture to *A Midsummer Night's Dream*, including the famous "Wedding March." WALTER LIBERACE, in subdued attire, appears as a soloist at age 17 with the Chicago Symphony Orchestra. BACH, age 17, competes successfully for the post of organist at the Jakobikirche, but the Duke of Weissenfels intervenes, making sure the job goes to an older man. Bach is probably bummed.

College freshman ROBERT ZIMMERMAN begins performing in Minnesota coffeehouses at age 18. A fan of Dylan Thomas, he calls himself Bob Dylan. PERCY BYSSHE SHELLEY, age 18, privately publishes a collection of poetry written with his sister and a Gothic horror novel called *Zastrozzi*. Injured while parachuting, JIMI HENDRIX gets out of the army. CHUBBY CHECKER, age 18, sings his number-one hit, "The Twist." SUSAN SONTAG receives her B.A. in philosophy from the University of Chicago at age 18. In Jamaica, BOB MARLEY, age 18, forms the first version of his reggae group, the Wailers.

MARY SHELLEY, age 19, competes with Byron and Shelley to write a ghost story. Only Mary finishes hers, *Frankenstein*, based on a nightmare. SERGEI RACHMANINOFF, age 19, writes his Prelude in C-sharp Minor, a piano piece so popular he is stuck playing it for the rest of his life. RICHARD HENRY DANA, age 19, suddenly leaves Harvard College to spend two years before the mast. From this experience, he will fashion one of the most popular nonfiction narratives in American literature. To avoid being mistaken for a Monkee, Davy Jones, age 19, changes his name to DAVID BOWIE.

PICASSO
enters his Blue Period.

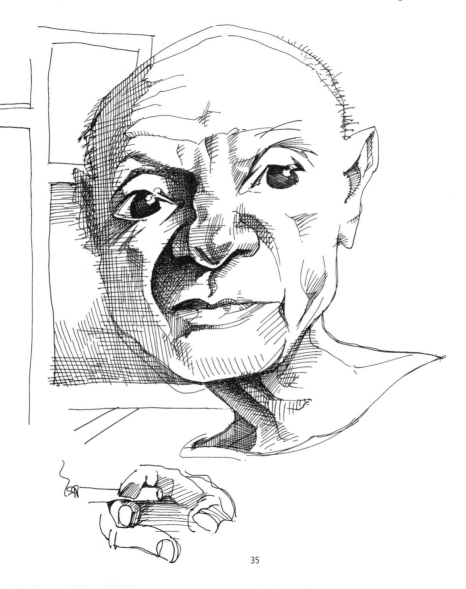

THE TWENTIES

HENRY DAVID THOREAU, age 20, quits his job as a teacher when he is ordered to use corporal punishment. Law student EDGAR DEGAS, age 20, persuades his father to let him study art instead. At age 20, PETER TOWNSHEND writes the lyrics, "Hope I die before I get old," but he doesn't. After opening for Elvis Presley, BUDDY HOLLY switches from country to rock 'n roll and records a number-one hit, "That'll Be the Day." SMOKEY ROBINSON, age 20, helps establish Motown and the Miracles with "Shop Around."

JACK LONDON, age 21, joins the Klondike gold rush and finds no gold but gathers plenty of material. NATHANIEL HAWTHORNE graduates from Bowdoin College at age 21, moves back into his mother's house, and stays there, almost reclusively, for the next twelve years. For a funerary architecture course at Yale, MAYA LIN, age 21, designs Washington's Vietnam Veterans Memorial. JOHN SINGER SARGENT exhibits his first portrait at the Paris Salon at age 21. GEORGE GERSHWIN, age 21, writes his first smash hit, "Swanee."

HERMAN MELVILLE
ships aboard the whaler *Acushnet*. Eventually, he'll get a book out of it.

While working at repairing railroad cars, F. SCOTT FITZGERALD, age 22, receives word that Scribner's is going to publish his first novel; he quits immediately. J. S. BACH, age 22, becomes the organist at Mühlhausen and marries his cousin. Marrying his cousin halts the career of JERRY LEE LEWIS: his cousin is thirteen, and at age 22 it's his third marriage. JAMES JOYCE, age 22, writes his first short story, "The Sisters," which is published as *Dubliners*. François-Marie Arouet, age 22, is thrown in the Bastille for writing offensive verses; while there, he changes his name to VOLTAIRE.

PAUL SIMON, age 22, drops out of law school and quits his job peddling songs to give performing another shot. Beach Boy BRIAN WILSON, age 22, suffers a nervous breakdown and decides to stay in his room. WYNTON MARSALIS, age 22, is the first artist ever to win Grammy awards for classical and jazz albums in the same year. JAMES BROWN, the godfather of soul at age 22, releases his first hit, "Please, Please, Please." RUDYARD KIPLING at age 22 publishes more than seventy short stories in seven paperback volumes.

RINGO STARR

agrees to shave his beard,
comb his hair forward,
and join the Beatles
for a salary of £25 a week.

Age TWENTY-TWO

WILLIAM WORDSWORTH, age 23, publishes his first and second collections of poetry. JOHN KEATS, in ode mode, writes "Ode to Psyche," "Ode to a Nightingale," and "Ode on a Grecian Urn" at age 23. AUGUST STRINDBERG, age 23, writes Sweden's first great play, *Mäster Olof*. R. CRUMB takes some bad acid at age 23 and creates everyone's favorite cartoon philosopher, Mr. Natural. HELEN KELLER graduates *cum laude* from Radcliffe College at age 23. ELVIS PRESLEY, age 23, enters the army. After six months of playing in piano bars, BILLY JOEL, age 23, writes "Piano Man."

Already a hit in England, JIMI HENDRIX, age 24, makes his first appearance in his native America and sets his guitar on fire. EVELYN WAUGH, age 24, publishes his first satiric novel, the very successful *Decline and Fall*. LANGSTON HUGHES, age 24, publishes his first volume of poetry, *The Weary Blues*. GOETHE, age 24, finishes writing *The Sorrows of Young Werther*, which makes his name known throughout Europe. JASPER JOHNS, American artist age 24, starts painting pictures of flags. MARCEL DUCHAMP, age 24, paints *Nude Descending a Staircase, No. 2*. British painter J. M. W. TURNER is elected an associate of the Royal Academy at the youngest possible age—24.

DAVID BOWIE
becomes
Ziggy Stardust.

49

Having worked as an engineer, a seaman, and a lumberjack, ALEXANDER CALDER, age 25, finally gives in and enrolls in New York City's Art Students League. THOMAS WOLFE, age 25, starts writing *Look Homeward, Angel.* TOULOUSE-LAUTREC, age 25, draws his first poster for the Moulin Rouge. ANTONIO VIVALDI, age 25, is ordained; known as the red-haired priest, he gives music lessons to orphan girls. To show his gratitude for being made an honorary member of Graz's music society, FRANZ SCHUBERT, age 25, sends an incomplete work; forty-three years later, Schubert's *Unfinished* Symphony receives its first performance.

WILLIAM FAULKNER, writing poetry and barely working at the post office, is described by his Uncle John, at age 26, as "not worth a Mississippi goddam." BO DIDDLEY, age 26, lends his name to his first single, which goes straight to the top of the R & B charts. GEORGES SEURAT, age 26, completes his pointillist masterpiece, *Sunday Afternoon on the Island of La Grande Jatte*. Five years after his mother gives him a box of oil paints, HENRI MATISSE makes his professional debut at age 26, sending four pictures to the Salon de la Société Nationale des Beaux-Arts.

EDGAR ALLAN POE
marries his
thirteen-year-old cousin, Virginia.
Quoth the raven, "Underage."

CHARLES SCHULZ, age 27, sells his idea for a comic strip called *Peanuts*. It appears in eight newspapers, and Snoopy acts like a real dog. MADONNA, age 27, makes two mistakes: marrying Sean Penn and co-starring with him in *Shanghai Express*. THOREAU, age 27, moves to Walden Pond, two miles outside of Concord, Massachusetts. EMILY BRONTË, age 27, writes her only novel, *Wuthering Heights*. It receives little recognition, and Emily dies within a year of its publication. MAN RAY, age 27, exhibits his *Self-Portrait*: two silent electric bells and a button on a black-and-aluminum background with his handprint as a signature. Even his friends don't see the likeness.

FYODOR DOSTOYEVSKY, age 28, is pardoned at the last minute and not shot to death for belonging to a political reform group. Having studied law at the University of Moscow, WASSILY KANDINSKY attends an exhibit of French impressionist paintings and decides at age 28 to become a painter. WOODY GUTHRIE, age 28, records his songs for the first time, thanks to Alan Lomax, a musicologist at the Library of Congress. Housewife ANNE SEXTON has a psychotic break at age 28, tries to kill herself, and starts writing poetry. KURT WEILL, age 28, composes *The Threepenny Opera*. ALBERT CAMUS, age 28, publishes *The Stranger*.

ALLEN GINSBERG
sits at a typewriter
and writes
"Howl,"
a poem that becomes
an icon of
the Beat generation.

Playwright CHRISTOPHER MARLOWE, age 29, argues over a tavern bill, gets stabbed above the eye, and dies. GLORIA STEINEM, age 29, goes undercover as a Playboy Bunny to write an exposé. MICHELANGELO, age 29, completes his statue of David. JAY MCINERNEY, age 29, publishes *Bright Lights, Big City*, which becomes a bestseller. PAUL MCCARTNEY, age 29, forms his second band with his wife and two guys named Denny. Norwegian artist EDVARD MUNCH creates *The Scream* at age 29.

In one night at age 29, FRANZ KAFKA writes "The Verdict" (the story, not the screenplay). PIET MONDRIAN, age 29, fails the figure-drawing test for the Dutch Prix de Rome. DOROTHY L. SAYERS, age 29, creates Lord Peter Wimsey for her first novel, *Whose Body?* MARK TWAIN, age 29, writes a funny story about a jumping frog and very quickly wins a national reputation as a humorist. BESSIE SMITH, age 29, releases her first record, "Gulf Coast Blues." Within six months, it sells 780,000 copies.

The Thirties

MARCEL DUCHAMP, age 30, displays a urinal at an art exhibition, calling it *Fountain* and signing it "R. Mutt." Challenged by his wife to write a better book than the English novel she's just read, JAMES FENIMORE COOPER, age 30, publishes *Precaution*. HELEN REDDY, age 30, sings her number-one hit anthem, "I Am Woman." SCOTT JOPLIN, age 30, publishes his "Maple Leaf Rag." NOËL COWARD, age 30, writes and stars in *Private Lives*, a glamorous smash hit the second it opens.

FRANZ KAFKA, age 30, publishes "Metamorphosis," in which a man wakes up one morning to find he has turned into a dung beetle. THORNTON WILDER, age 30, finishes *The Bridge of San Luis Rey*, which wins the Pulitzer Prize and propels him into national celebrity. ROBERT LOUIS STEVENSON writes the opening installment of *Treasure Island* at age 30. COUNT BASIE, age 30, forms his first jazz band.

CYNDI LAUPER
releases her first solo album,
which includes
"Girls Just
Want to Have Fun."

FRANZ SCHUBERT writes a piano duet, a symphony, a mass, nine songs, and then dies at the age of 31, probably from syphilis. RICHARD WRIGHT, age 31, publishes his first novel, *Native Son*. ERICA JONG, age 31, publishes *Fear of Flying*. ANDRÉ MALRAUX, age 31, writes *Man's Fate*. MANET breaks through to a personal, original style at age 31 and is rejected by the Salon of 1863, thus gaining a reputation as a rebel. After suffering a nervous breakdown, jazz singer JOE WILLIAMS, age 31, quits singing to sell Fuller brushes.

RICHARD WAGNER, age 32, composes his first really successful opera, *Tannhäuser*. WILLIAM FAULKNER'S fourth novel, *The Sound and the Fury*, despite excellent reviews, sells fewer than 2,000 copies. Faulkner, age 32, works the night shift at a power plant to pay his bills. JEAN-PAUL SARTRE, age 32, picks a nice title for his first novel—*Nausea*. Thanks to his success with *The Spy Who Came in from the Cold*, David Cornwell resigns from the British foreign service at age 32 and devotes his time to writing as JOHN LE CARRÉ.

THEODOR GEISEL,
under the name Dr. Seuss,
publishes a children's book,
*And to Think That I Saw It
on Mulberry Street.*

GEORGE ORWELL, age 33, goes to Spain to help fight Franco's fascists. To pay for the trip, he pawns his share of the family silver. CLAES OLDENBURG, age 33, makes his first soft sculptures: a giant slice of cake, an ice cream cone, and a hamburger. LEWIS CARROLL, age 33, publishes *Alice's Adventures in Wonderland*. T. S. ELIOT, age 33, writes *The Waste Land*. EDWARD LEAR, age 33, is summoned by Queen Victoria, age twenty-seven, to give her drawing lessons. He also publishes his first book of limericks.

P. G. WODEHOUSE

introduces
Jeeves and Wooster
to the world.
The world is pleased.

PAUL GAUGUIN, age 34, abandons his career as a stockbroker to become a painter. When *Five Weeks in a Balloon* is accepted for publication, JULES VERNE, also age 34, also quits stock-broking. Former commercial artist ANDY WARHOL, age 34, becomes an artist when he exhibits his paintings of Campbell's soup cans. EDWARD ALBEE, age 34, has his first smash hit on Broadway, *Who's Afraid of Virginia Woolf?* BEETHOVEN, at age 34, manages to write his only opera, *Fidelio*. It's not bad. After a suicide attempt, CHARLIE PARKER, age 34, checks into Bellevue. When he gets out, he plays at Birdland for the last time before his tragically early demise.

SINCLAIR LEWIS, age 35, turns in the manuscript of his satire on small-town America, *Main Street*. In six months, it sells 180,000 copies. MOZART, in the last year of his life, composes a clarinet concerto, a string quintet, two operas, and an unfinished requiem. Ten years after thumbing his way across the country, JACK KEROUAC, age 35, reads in the *New York Times* that his new novel, *On the Road*, is "an authentic work of art . . . a major novel." JACKSON POLLOCK, age 35, begins dripping paint directly onto his canvases. WILLIAM HOGARTH, age 35, publishes his first series of satirical, narrative pictures, *The Harlot's Progress*.

*After arguing with
Gauguin,*
VINCENT VAN GOGH
slices off his ear
and takes it to a brothel,
asking that it be given
to Rachel.

JELLY ROLL MORTON
cooks up his
Red Hot Peppers.

Having tried his hand at being a cowboy, a miner, and a railroad detective, EDGAR RICE BURROUGHS, age 36, decides to take a whack at writing. His first story is published under the pseudonym "Normal Bean." With 36 cents in her pocket, TINA TURNER, age 36, sneaks out of a hotel and escapes from her abusive husband, Ike. THOMAS WOLFE, age 36, goes home again, but then discovers that you can't. GEORGES BIZET, age 36, composes his most famous opera, *Carmen*. It runs to thirty-seven performances, but on the day of the thirty-first, Bizet dies of a throat infection.

BAUDELAIRE, age 36, publishes *Les Fleurs du Mal* and is tried for offenses against religion and public decency. OSCAR WILDE, age 36, publishes his first (and only) novel, *The Picture of Dorian Gray*, which meets with immediate success. WILLIAM BLAKE, age 36, illustrates and publishes *Songs of Experience*, which includes "Tyger! Tyger! burning bright." A former detective himself, DASHIELL HAMMETT, age 36, publishes *The Maltese Falcon*, featuring tough guy Sam Spade. A successful business writer, AMY TAN, age 36, publishes her first fiction, *The Joy Luck Club*.

JAMES MCNEILL WHISTLER, age 37, paints his mom. Attorney SCOTT TUROW, age 37, finishes *Presumed Innocent*, the novel he has been writing on the train while commuting to and from the office. VINCENT VAN GOGH paints his last painting, *Cornfield with Crows*, and shoots himself at age 37. MARCEL PROUST, age 37, bites a madeleine, sips his tea, and gets the inspiration for how to approach his seven-volume novel, *Remembrance of Things Past*. MICHELANGELO, age 37, finishes painting the ceiling of the Sistine Chapel. With absolutely no knowledge of the Lone Ranger, GIOACCHINO ROSSINI, age 37, writes *William Tell*, his fortieth and last opera.

In his editor's office, ERNEST HEMINGWAY, age 38, encounters a critic who has called his *Death in the Afternoon* "Bull in the Afternoon." Hemingway smacks him with a copy of the critic's own book and then heads for Spain to cover the civil war. Eight years after he started writing it, JOSEPH HELLER, age 38, finally publishes *Catch 22*. RALPH ELLISON, age 38, publishes his great, but only, novel, *Invisible Man*. DAVE BRUBECK'S quartet records "Take Five," the first jazz single to go gold. RALPH WALDO EMERSON, age 38, gains fame with the publication of his first book on transcendentalism, *Essays*.

JOHN CAGE

writes 4'33",
a composition for piano
consisting of
four minutes and
thirty-three seconds
of silence.

Iowan GRANT WOOD, age 39, paints *American Gothic*.
International singing star JULIO IGLESIAS makes his
first album in English at age 39. Postal inspector ANTHONY
TROLLOPE, age 39, writes *The Warden*. PEARL S. BUCK,
age 39, writes *The Good Earth*, which wins her a Pulitzer Prize and
a Nobel Prize. LEONARD BERNSTEIN, age 39, writes the
groundbreaking music for *West Side Story*. WILLA CATHER,
age 39, publishes her first successful novel, *O Pioneers!* CAMILLE
SAINT-SAËNS, age 39, composes his symphonic poem, *Danse
Macabre*. GABRIEL GÁRCIA MÁRQUEZ, age 39,
publishes *One Hundred Years of Solitude*.

THE FORTIES

FORGING
AHEAD

FRÉDÉRIC-AUGUSTE BARTHOLDI, age 40, starts
a really big project: his statue for New York Harbor, "Liberty
Enlightening the World." Without ever having learned to read
music, JULIO IGLESIAS, age 40, makes the *Guinness Book
of World Records* as the world's best-selling recording artist, with
over 100 million albums sold. After seven years of writing,
JAMES JOYCE, age 40, publishes *Ulysses* on his birthday.
LIBERACE, age 40, wins his libel suit against a London
newspaper and one of its columnists who has insinuated he is
a homosexual.

On his 40th birthday, ROY LICHTENSTEIN reads in the *New York Times* that he is "one of the worst artists in America." Nevertheless, he is invited to create works for the New York State pavilion at the World's Fair. OSCAR WILDE, age 40, attends the opening of his last play, *The Importance of Being Earnest*; he is also found guilty of indecency and sodomy and sentenced to two years of hard labor in prison. With his wife Yoko Ono, JOHN LENNON, age 40, releases *Double Fantasy* with its number-one hit, "Just Like Starting Over." Three weeks later, he encounters a crazed fan in front of the Dakota.

SALMAN RUSHDIE, age 41, goes into hiding when the Ayatollah Khomeini puts a bounty on his head for writing *The Satanic Verses*: $2.6 million if an Iranian kills him, $1 million for anyone else. BING CROSBY, age 41, spends eighteen minutes in the studio recording "White Christmas." His version sells over 30 million copies. While crossing the Atlantic, successful painter SAMUEL F. B. MORSE, age 41, conceives of the telegraph. RUDYARD KIPLING, age 41, receives the Nobel Prize for Literature, the first English author to win it.

Nine years after he began writing it, HENRY MILLER, age 42, publishes *Tropic of Cancer*. GEORGE ORWELL, age 42, sees the publication of his political fable, *Animal Farm*. PAUL GAUGUIN, age 42, leaves Paris and goes to live with the natives in Tahiti. CAMILLE PAGLIA, age 42, steps into the spotlight with her first book, *Sexual Personae*, a revision of her dissertation that was rejected by seven publishers. Jazz pianist THELONIOUS MONK, age 42, finally gains international recognition with his quartet.

*Less than a month
before his death,*
ELVIS
performs live for the
last time, in Indianapolis.

THOMAS GAINSBOROUGH, age 43, exhibits his painting, *The Blue Boy*. TCHAIKOVSKY, slogging through a creative trench at age 43, writes a suite whose third movement features ad lib accordians. BETTE MIDLER, age 43, sings her first number-one hit, "Wind Beneath My Wings." HENRI MATISSE, age 43, gets some good publicity when his painting *Blue Nude* is burned in effigy in Chicago. BRAHMS, age 43, finally finishes his first symphony, begun twenty-one years earlier. ANTOINE DE SAINT-EXUPÉRY, age 43, writes his best-known work, *The Little Prince*.

Successful playwright and author A. A. MILNE, age 44, writes a book about a stuffed bear named Winnie-the-Pooh. Blues master B. B. KING, age 44, has his first and only Top Twenty single, "The Thrill Is Gone." CLEMENT C. MOORE, a professor of Oriental and Greek literature at New York City's General Theological Seminary, writes *A Visit from St. Nicholas* at age 44. LEONARDO DA VINCI, age 44, paints the *Last Supper* on the wall of a monastery. Newspaper editor FRANK BAUM, age 44, publishes *The Wonderful Wizard of Oz*, first of fourteen books.

MARVIN GAYE
argues violently with his father,
an Apostolic preacher,
who shoots
and kills him.

ÉMILE ZOLA, age 45, writes his masterpiece, *Germinal*.
BONNIE RAITT, age 45, becomes the first woman to have
a guitar named after her, Fender's "Bonnie Raitt Signature Series
Strato-caster." NATHANIEL HAWTHORNE, age 45,
publishes his first major novel to fine reviews, *The Scarlet Letter*.
Despite a deadly case of tuberculosis, GEORGE ORWELL,
age 45, manages to finish his last novel, *Nineteen Eighty-four*.
J. R. R. TOLKIEN, age 45, publishes *The Hobbit* and
starts writing *The Lord of the Rings*. CHUCK BERRY,
age 45, releases "My Ding-a-Ling." For some reason, it becomes
his first hit in years.

CHER, age 46, re-records "I Got You Babe," this time with Beavis and Butthead. NORMAN MAILER, age 46, runs for mayor of New York city on a platform calling for the city to become America's fifty-first state and loses. ARNOLD SCHOENBERG, age 46, discovers twelve-tone musical composition. SAMUEL JOHNSON, age 46, completes his massive dictionary of the English language. Editor and teacher TONI MORRISON, age 46, publishes her breakthrough novel, *Song of Solomon*. ROBERT FROST co-founds the Bread Loaf School of English at Middlebury College at age 46.

With the success of *Waiting for Godot*, SAMUEL BECKETT, age 47, gets his first taste of success and doesn't much like it. REX STOUT, age 47, publishes his first detective novel, introducing Nero Wolfe. NOAH WEBSTER, age 47, publishes his first dictionary. AUGUSTE RODIN, age 47, sculpts *The Thinker*. Having deliberately set out to write a best-seller, MARIO PUZO, age 48, succeeds wildly with *The Godfather*. PETER TOWNSHEND, age 48, wins a Tony for *Tommy*.

KATE CHOPIN, age 48, shocks the American public with her novel, *The Awakening*. Two thousand characters and ninety volumes after he began, BALZAC, age 48, writes the last of *The Human Comedy*. NEIL YOUNG, age 49, collaborates with Pearl Jam on *Mirror Ball*. ERIC CLAPTON, age 49, releases *From the Cradle*, which becomes the best-selling traditional blues recording in history. CHARLES DICKENS, age 49, finishes writing *Great Expectations* but then changes the ending to suit his publisher.

FRANK ZAPPA
serves as Czechoslovakia's
liaison to the West for trade,
tourism, and culture.

THE FIFTIES

SECOND
WIND

*With the rock era
rolling along,*
FRANK SINATRA
has a number-one hit,
"Strangers in the Night."

With the premiere of his eighth symphony, GUSTAV MAHLER, age 50, enjoys his first unqualified success as a composer. SELMA LAGERLÖF, age 50, wins the Nobel Prize for Literature, the first woman to do so. At President Clinton's inauguration, ARETHA FRANKLIN, age 50, wears a fur coat and sings a song from *Les Misérables.* HERMANN HESSE, age 50, publishes *Steppenwolf.* STEVE "SPACE COWBOY" MILLER, age 50, takes his band on the road to fifty cities.

Unitarian minister ROBERT FULGHUM, age 51, writes his first book, a bestseller *All I Really Need to Know I Learned in Kindergarten*, which includes a description of a perfect grandfather, even though Fulghum never knew his. BARBRA STREISAND, age 51, sings to a paying live audience for the first time in twenty-two years. Former oil executive RAYMOND CHANDLER, age 51, publishes his first hard-boiled book, *The Big Sleep*. Playwright HENRIK IBSEN, age 51, writes *A Doll's House*.

LEONARDO DA VINCI
starts a new painting, the *Mona Lisa*.

DOMENICO SCARLATTI, age 52, publishes his first collection of the six hundred harpsichord sonatas he eventually composes. TCHAIKOVSKY, age 52, finishes his ballet, *The Nutcracker*. GEORGE ELIOT, age 52, publishes her masterpiece, *Middlemarch*. Reclusive author THOMAS PYNCHON, age 52, publishes his first novel in sixteen years, *Vineland*, still without his photo on the jacket. IRVING BERLIN, age 52, writes "the best song I ever wrote" and "the best song anybody ever wrote"—"White Christmas."

ERNEST HEMINGWAY, age 53, publishes *The Old Man and the Sea.* Painter PETER PAUL RUBENS, age 53, doubles as a diplomat, helping to arrange a peace treaty between Spain and England, for which he is knighted, and marries his second wife, who is sixteen. FRANZ LISZT, age 53, receives minor orders from the Roman Catholic Church and gets to call himself "Abbé." After a career as a lawyer and a Civil War soldier, GENERAL LEW WALLACE, age 53, writes *Ben-Hur.* Although completely deaf, BEETHOVEN, age 53, finishes his magnificent Ninth Symphony.

While trying to kick his heroin addiction,

JERRY GARCIA

truly becomes one of the Dead; whether he is grateful remains unknown.

LUIGI PIRANDELLO, age 54, writes the first of his plays to capture the public's attention, *Six Characters in Search of an Author*. HECTOR BERLIOZ, age 54, completes his masterpiece, *The Trojans*, but the Paris Opera turns it down; in his lifetime, it gets only one, terribly abridged, production.

TOM WOLFE, age 55, publishes his first novel, *The Bonfire of the Vanities*, and begins telling people how to write novels. PICASSO, age 55, paints his famous reaction to the destruction of a Basque town in the Spanish Civil War, *Guernica*. After thirteen rejections, WILLIAM KENNEDY, age 55, finally gets his novel, *Ironweed*, published. Violin virtuoso PAGANINI, age 55, tries to open a gambling casino in Paris but fails. Having managed to get *The Gulag Archipelago* published in Paris, SOLZHENITSYN, age 55, is exiled from the U.S.S.R.

MARK TWAIN
learns to ride a bicycle.

DANTE, age 56, completes *The Divine Comedy*. HANDEL, age 56, composes the *Messiah*. E. ANNIE PROULX, age 56, publishes her first novel, *Postcards*, and wins the PEN/Faulkner Award for Fiction, the first woman to do so. VLADIMIR NABOKOV, age 56, publishes his notorious novel, *Lolita*. CERVANTES, age 57, publishes *Don Quixote*. Twelve years after starting, J. R. R. TOLKIEN, age 57, finishes writing *The Lord of the Rings*; six more years pass before it is published. LEO TOLSTOY, age 57, gives up meat, alcohol, cigarettes, white bread, and hunting, but keeps on writing.

JONATHAN SWIFT, age 58, publishes *Gulliver's Travels*.
Virtuoso pianist IGNACY PADEREWSKI becomes the
prime minister of Poland at age 58. With his poodle Charlie,
JOHN STEINBECK, age 58, sets out in a camper in search
of America; the result, *Travels with Charlie*, wins him the Nobel
Prize. JOHNNY MATHIS, age 58, sells out three concerts
at Carnegie Hall. JOHN MILTON, age 58, publishes his epic
poem, *Paradise Lost*. Thirty years after creating him, JOHN
UPDIKE, age 58, kills off Harry "Rabbit" Angstrom in *Rabbit
at Rest*.

DANIEL DEFOE, age 59, publishes his first novel, *Robinson Crusoe*. IKE TURNER, age 59, is unable to attend his induction into the Rock and Roll Hall of Fame because he's in prison for possession of cocaine. SUSAN SONTAG, age 59, publishes her first novel in twenty-five years, *The Volcano Lover*. Two months before his death, DOSTOYEVSKY, age 59, completes *The Brothers Karamazov*.

SONNY BONO

becomes a
U.S. congressman.

THE SIXTIES

HITTING
TOP
SPEED

JOHN GUTZON BORGLUM, age 60, starts carving Mt. Rushmore. Years after getting the idea, CHRISTO, age 60, finally wraps the German Reichstag. RAY CHARLES, age 60, sings "You got the right one, baby—uh, huh!" for Diet Pepsi. VICTOR HUGO, age 60, publishes *Les Misérables* without getting the rights to any future musical versions. EDWARD HOPPER'S *Nighthawks* is shown at the Art Institute of Chicago and wins a $750 prize.

KURT VONNEGUT, JR., age 61, fails where his mother suc-

ceeded: he tries to commit suicide. WILLIAM FAULKNER,

age 61, fervently takes up a new sport: riding to hounds, chasing the fox.

JACQUES OFFENBACH, age 61, saves his greatest (and

his ninetieth) operetta, *The Tales of Hoffmann*, for the very end: he is

working on it at his death. HENRIK IBSEN, age 62, writes

Hedda Gabler. CARDINAL FRANCIS JOSEPH

SPELLMAN, the archbishop of New York, writes a best-selling

novel, *The Foundling*, at age 62.

AGATHA CHRISTIE
turns her story
"Three Blind Mice" into a play,
The Mousetrap, which runs for
over forty years.

REMBRANDT, age 63, paints his last self-portrait. After years as an obscure poet, ROBERT BLY, age 63, hops onto the bestseller lists with *Iron John*, a book about the needs of American men. THOMAS HOBBES, age 63, publishes his major work, *Leviathan*. JOHNNY CASH, age 63, teams up with Kris Kristofferson, Waylon Jennings, and Willie Nelson to record *The Road Goes On Forever*.

FATS DOMINO releases his first major-label album in twenty-five years, *Christmas Is a Special Day*. KINGSLEY AMIS, age 64, publishes *The Old Devils*, a comic study of early old age. Impoverished, BÉLA BARTÓK, age 64, leaves his third piano concerto unfinished and dies of leukemia in a New York City hospital. In the last year of his life, EDVARD GRIEG, age 64, revises his one piano concerto, which remains extremely popular. PUCCINI, age 65, finishes all but one duet and one scene of *Turandot* and then dies. JOSEPH HAYDN, age 65, writes Austria's national anthem.

GEORGIA O'KEEFFE
goes to Europe for the first time;
unable to speak French,
she refuses to meet Picasso.

TONY BENNETT, age 66, achieves certified hipness
all over again, presenting an MTV Music Video award alongside
Flea of the Red Hot Chili Peppers. Seven years after he began,
PAUL CÉZANNE, age 66, completes his painting, *Bathers*;
oblivious (naturally) to his posthumous fame, he works on in
relative obscurity. After twenty years of interrupted writing,
BORIS PASTERNAK, age 66, completes *Doctor Zhivago*,
but the Soviet authorities refuse publication.

SIR RICHARD BURTON, age 67, publishes the tenth and final volume of his famous translation of the Arabian classic, *The Book of the Thousand Nights and a Night*. At an Eric Clapton concert, MUDDY WATERS, age 67, plays his blues guitar one more time. KURT VONNEGUT, JR., age 67, publishes his thirteenth novel, *Hocus Pocus*.

In two hours, as the client drives
from Milwaukee to his studio,

FRANK LLOYD
WRIGHT

quickly designs the house called
Fallingwater, about which the
client, pleased, says,
"Don't change a thing."

HENRY ADAMS, age 68, finishes his autobiography, *The Education of Henry Adams*, which will turn out to be his best-known work. For an edition of the *Book of Job*, WILLIAM BLAKE, age 68, provides what will prove to be some of his most famous illustrations. Thirty-three years after winning a Grammy for "I Left My Heart in San Francisco," TONY BENNETT, age 68, picks up a couple more for his *Unplugged* album.

JOHN CAGE, age 69, presents *A House Full of Music* using eight hundred schoolchildren. IGOR STRAVINSKY, age 69, conducts the premiere of his new opera, *The Rake's Progress*. RICHARD WAGNER, age 69, completes his last opera, *Parsifal*.

THE SEVENTIES

ANOTHER KIND OF PRIME TIME

WILLIAM WORDSWORTH, age 70, hikes up a local peak and comes down with new sonnets in his head, including a sequence on capital punishment. E. M. FORSTER, age 70, writes his first libretto, for Benjamin Britten's *Billy Budd*. W. SOMERSET MAUGHAM, age 70, publishes *The Razor's Edge*, which achieves greater immediate success than any of his previous novels. ANDREW WYETH, age 70, sets the art world buzzing with speculation about the identity of "Helga" when he exhibits several paintings of her.

COLETTE, age 71, publishes another book about a young girl, *Gigi*. PIET MONDRIAN, age 71, shows his final masterpiece, a new departure from his black lines, called *Broadway Boogie Woogie*. Shortly before his death, DOMENICO SCARLATTI, age 71, manages to dash off a *Salve Regina* for soprano and strings. To reduce his taxes, HENRY MILLER, age 71, churns out one hundred and fifteen watercolors in five months for charitable contributions. Author AMBROSE BIERCE, age 71, wanders off to Mexico and disappears.

*Against all expectations,
hard-drinking poet*
CHARLES BUKOWSKI
lives to see the publication
of his collection,
Septuagenarian Stew.

Coaxed out of retirement by a new libretticist, GIUSEPPE VERDI, age 72, writes *Otello*. ANSEL ADAMS, age 72, makes his first trip to Europe and has a major exhibition of his photographs at the Met. DIZZY GILLESPIE, age 72, makes his debut as a dramatic actor, playing a disillusioned jazz musician in *The Winter in Lisbon*. Although nearly blind, HANDEL, age 72, writes his twenty-first oratorio, *The Triumph of Time and Truth*. WALT WHITMAN publishes his ninth and final version of *Leaves of Grass*.

WORDSWORTH, age 73, becomes England's Poet

Laureate. After being excommunicated by the Orthodox Church,

TOLSTOY, age 73, writes *What Is Religion?* and starts

rereading Shakespeare. EDWARD LEAR, age 73, writes

his last poem, a nonsense auto-obituary called "Incidents in the

Life of My Uncle Arly."

While interviewing Federico Fellini on *Casanova*, GEORGES SIMENON, age 74, remarks that he has had sex with 10,000 women, 8,000 of them prostitutes, which makes world headlines. Still able to play only in F-sharp major (the black keys), IRVING BERLIN, age 74, hauls his transposing piano out of storage to write his eighteenth musical, *Mr. President*. Virtuoso pianist FRANZ LISZT, age 74, gives his final concert twelve days before his death. WILLIAM CARLOS WILLIAMS, a physician for over forty years, completes his best-known poem, *Paterson*, at age 74.

Having just won a Pulitzer Prize and a National Book Award,

poet WALLACE STEVENS, unwilling to retire from the

insurance business, refuses a Harvard professorship at age 75.

JOHN CAGE presents *Europera*, a montage of fragments,

saying, "For 200 years, the Europeans have been sending us their

operas. Now I'm sending them back."

Because of her arthritis, GRANDMA MOSES, age 76,

gives up embroidery and begins to paint. In the last year of his life,

ROSSINI, age 76, continues working on a collection of piano

pieces called *Sins of Old Age.* A book of NORMAN

ROCKWELL'S paintings, published when he is 76, sells

57,000 copies in six weeks at sixty bucks a pop.

HENRI MATISSE, age 77, publishes *Jazz*, a book on art and life illustrated with his own brightly colored paper cutouts. At age 77, FRANK SINATRA'S new album, *Duets*, debuts at number two on the charts. THOMAS HARDY, age 77, publishes his poetry collection, *Moments of Vision*, a critical success. For Memorial Day, AARON COPLAND, age 78, conducts the National Symphony on the grounds of the Capitol in Washington, D.C. Confined to a wheelchair by rheumatoid arthritis, RENOIR, age 78, keeps painting.

JOHN CAGE

composes pieces for cello,
for Scottish folk band,
and for one or two pianos,
twelve rainsticks, violin or
oscillator, and silence.

After a long hiatus, GIUSEPPE VERDI, age 79, writes a comic opera, *Falstaff*, which remains popular. GRANDMA MOSES, age 79, has her first show of art in New York City. Nobel laureate THOMAS MANN, age 79, publishes his last novel, *The Confessions of Felix Krull, Confidence Man*.

After twenty years,
MARCEL DUCHAMP
finishes his last startling work of
art, *Given: 1. the waterfall,*
2. the illuminating gas.

THE EIGHTIES

FOR THE INTREPID
ONLY

VOLTAIRE, age 80, spends most of his time in his library of

over 6,000 volumes, writing some forty pieces (historical essays,

a tragedy, and his three last tales) and administering the hundred or

so houses he owns. In his thirty-third year as conductor of the Berlin

Philharmonic, HERBERT VON KARAJAN, age 80,

celebrates his sixtieth year of conducting. HENRY MILLER,

age 80, studies silk-screen printing with the nuns at Hollywood's

Immaculate Heart College. RICHARD STRAUSS, age 80,

composes his Sonatina Number 2 in E-flat Major for sixteen wind

instruments.

GEORGE BERNARD SHAW, age 80, gives up driving, but keeps walking (up to six miles at a stretch) and tries improving Shakespeare in his *Cymbeline Refinished*. After the death of his wife, TOLKIEN, age 80, moves back to Oxford, where he receives an honorary Doctorate of Letters and continues working on *The Silmarillion*, begun fifty-five years before. TENNYSON, age 80, publishes *Demeter and Other Poems*, which sells 20,000 copies in the first week. W. SOMERSET MAUGHAM, age 80, revises an earlier book and offers it as *Ten Novels and Their Authors*, to huge advance sales.

CLAUDE MONET,
ill and virtually blind from
cataracts, begins a series of
twelve large paintings of
water lilies.

HENRI MATISSE, age 81, finishes completely decorating a Dominican chapel, including stained glass windows, murals, vestments, and liturgical objects. E. M. FORSTER, age 81, testifies in court against banning D. H. Lawrence's *Lady Chatterly's Lover*.

GOETHE, age 82, completes his masterpiece, *Faust*. After an absence of sixty-one years, VLADIMIR HOROWITZ, age 82, plays a triumphant piano recital in Russia. BENJAMIN FRANKLIN, age 82, finishes his famous autobiography. SAMUEL BECKETT, age 82, publishes his last work, *Stirrings Still*, a fiction of fewer than 2,000 words.

Tired of fighting with his wife,

TOLSTOY

leaves her, sneaking out of
the house in the middle of the night.
He takes his diary with him
and describes his
escape but dies ten days later.

GRAHAM GREENE, age 83, publishes his twenty-fourth novel, *The Captain and the Enemy.* VLADIMIR HOROWITZ, age 83, plays the piano in a newly refurbished Carnegie Hall. Afterwards, he announces backstage that the hall's acoustics have been ruined and that he will never play there again. And he doesn't. Suffering from writer's cramp, W. SOMERSET MAUGHAM, age 84, finishes his essay collection *Points of View* wearing a surgical glove. VERDI, age 84, composes four sacred choral works: *Stabat Mater*, *Te Deum*, *Laudi alla Vergine Maria*, and *Ave Maria.*

DAME AGATHA CHRISTIE, age 85, writes her sixty-sixth mystery novel. Sculptor HENRY MOORE, age 85, has a major exhibition of his work at New York City's Metropolitan Museum of Art. CARL SANDBURG, age 85, publishes *Honey and Salt*, including poems that some critics consider his best. HERMANN HESSE, age 85, revises a poem, listens to a Mozart sonata, goes to bed, and dies in his sleep.

ROBERT FROST
recites at Kennedy's presidential inauguration, the first poet to ever do so.

TOSCANINI, age 86, conducts his last concert, an all-Wagner program, from Carnegie Hall. PICASSO, age 86, begins a new series of etchings. In Jackson, Mississippi, a few blocks from where she grew up, EUDORA WELTY, age 86, receives the French Legion of Honor medal. Four days before his death, VLADIMIR HOROWITZ, age 86, completes his last recording, including Liszt's arrangement of Bach's *Liebestod*.

GEORGE BERNARD SHAW, age 87, visits the set of the film *Caesar and Cleopatra*, based on his play, and poses for pictures wearing a Roman helmet. He also advises the filmmakers on the score and other details, including the pitch of one character's death scream. PICASSO, age 87, begins a new series of etchings. TOSCANINI, age 87, conducts his last concert, an all-Wagner program, from Carnegie Hall.

ARTUR RUBINSTEIN, age 88, gives twelve piano concerts in America and fifteen in Europe. REX STOUT, age 88, writes his last Nero Wolfe mystery. FRANK LLOYD WRIGHT, age 89, offers Chicago his design for an office building a mile high—four times as tall as the Empire State Building—with atomic-powered elevators. Chicago passes. Despite her failing vision, GEORGIA O'KEEFFE, age 89, begins a new series of oil paintings, *From a Day with Juan.*

CRUISING TOWARD THE CENTURY

In mourning for Euripides,
SOPHOCLES
appears with his chorus
and actors at the dress parade
before the Great Dionysia.

THOMAS HOBBES, age 90, writes a poem with the lines, "Yet I can love and have a mistress too/As fair as can be and as wise as fair." ANDRÉS SEGOVIA, age 90, still travels the world, playing over fifty concerts a year on his classical guitar. LEOPOLD STOKOWSKI, age 90, re-creates his debut with the London Symphony orchestra sixty years before, conducting Wagner's prelude to *Die Meistersinger von Nürnberg.*

Finnish composer JEAN SIBELIUS, age 91, not having published a composition in twenty-seven years, remarks, "When one takes one's leave of life, one notices how much one has left undone." MAUGHAM, age 91, wakes up on his birthday and says, "Oh, hell, another birthday." FRANK LLOYD WRIGHT, age 91, continues work on the Marin County government center and several other projects, and also accepts another commission.

GEORGE BERNARD SHAW, age 92, writes a post-atomic fantasy called *Farfetched Fables* and accepts a commission to write a ten-minute puppet play, which he does in four days. P. G. WODEHOUSE, age 92, writes his last Jeeves and Wooster story. He also writes, "If only I had taken up golf earlier and devoted my whole time to it instead of fooling about writing stories and things, I might have got my handicap down to under eighteen." BERTRAND RUSSELL, age 92, writes an article for *Playboy*, on "Semantics and the Cold War."

Cellist PABLO CASALS, age 93, begins each day as he has for eighty years: he plays two Bach preludes and fugues on the piano. LEOPOLD STOKOWSKI, age 93, has a new home built for himself on the Riviera. P. G. WODEHOUSE, age 93, works on another comic novel right up to the end. *Sunset at Blandings* is his ninety-sixth book or so. SHAW, age 94, releases his final work for publication, Bernard Shaw's Rhyming Picture Guide to Ayot (the town where he lived his last years).

New contract in hand, STOKOWSKI, age 95, heads back into the studio to record the symphony Bizet wrote when he was seventeen. Jazz pianist EUBIE BLAKE, age 95, plays on the White House lawn for a celebration of the Newport Jazz Festival's twenty-fifth anniversary (begun back when Eubie was a mere lad of seventy). He steals the show. BERTRAND RUSSELL, age 96, writes his final harumph against religion for publication in *The Humanist*, saying "My views on religion remain those which I acquired at the age of sixteen. I consider all forms of religion not only false but harmful."

MARC CHAGALL, age 97, continues to paint, exhibiting such works as *The Dream* and *Back to Back*. Still overseeing his own business affairs, IRVING BERLIN, age 98, refuses to let ASCAP buy a full-page advertisement in the *New York Times* in honor of his upcoming birthday, saying, "I pay you to administer my money, not squander it." EUBIE BLAKE, age 99, still accepts paying gigs.

*After the celebrations for her
100th birthday,*
GRANDMA MOSES
goes back to work and completes
twenty-five more paintings.
She has enjoyed a quarter century
of being an artist.

INDEX

INDEX

At age 6, DAVID LEWMAN sang on a series of records called *Let's Learn to Sing*. At age 35, he made his off-Broadway debut alongside George Wendt in a quasi-musical called *Wild Men*. At his current age (which he cannot disclose, as he recently moved to Los Angeles), he wrote this book. He has also written articles for *Nickelodeon* magazine, *Inside Chicago*, *Online Access*, and *Chicago Times*.

MARK ANDERSON illustrates and designs publications for a number of national and international clients. His illustrations have appeared in *Outside* magazine, *Chicago Magazine*, the *Chicago Tribune* and the *Washingtonian*. At age 33, this is his first book.